D1263880

THE HIPPOPOTAMUS

ESSENTIAL POETS SERIES 117

Guernica Editions Inc. acknowledges the support of
the Raiziss-Giop Charitable Foundation.
Guernica Editions Inc. acknowledges the support of the Istituto Italiano
di Cultura, Chicago (Director: Francesca Valente).

LUCIANO ERBA

THE HIPPOPOTAMUS

TRANSLATED BY ANN SNODGRASS

GUERNICA

TORONTO·BUFFALO·CHICAGO·LANCASTER (U.K.)

2003

Antonio D'Alfonso, editor
Guernica Editions Inc.
P.O. Box 117, Station P, Toronto (ON), Canada M5S 2S6
2250 Military Road, Tonawanda, N.Y. 14150-6000 U.S.A.

Distributors:
University of Toronto Press Distribution,
5201 Dufferin Street, Toronto, (ON), Canada M3H 5T8

Gazelle Book Services, Falcon House, Queen Square,
Lancaster LA1 1RN U.K.

Independent Publishers Group,
814 N. Franklin Street, Chicago, Il. 60610 U.S.A.

First edition.
Printed in Canada.

Legal Deposit – First Quarter.
National Library of Canada.
Library of Congress Catalog Card Number: 2002113556.
National Library of Canada Cataloguing in Publication
Erba, Luciano, 1922-
The hippopotamus / Luciano Erba ; translated by Ann Snodgrass.
(Essential poets series ; 117)
Translation of: L'ippopotamo.
Text in English and Italian.
ISBN 1-55071-157-1
I. Snodgrass, Ann. II. Title. III. Series.
PQ4865.R316713 2002   851'.914   C2002-904865-6

Contents

III. Elsewhere

Acknowledgements

Many thanks to the editors of the following journals in which many of these poems have appeared: *Orion*: "In the Woods," "Ending Vacations," "Irreversibility"; *Quarterly West*: "American Suite," *Salamander*: "Self-Portrait," "Metaphysical Streetcar Conductor"; *Verse*: "City and Bridge"; *Yale Italian Poetry*: "Istria," "Wire," "In Romagna," "Clouds."

I

THE OPEN HOOP

To M.

se mai ti ricorderò come una madonna senese
tu cosí bruna, poco ovale, assai illirica
sarà che a volte nel segreto degli occhi
passò una luce d'immensa dolcezza
e tanto bastò perché apparisse un ciel d'oro
di pietà, di letizia sulla selva dei tuoi capelli

If I Ever

If I ever remember you as a Sienese madonna
you so auburn, almost oval, deeply illyrian
it will be because at times in the secret of your eyes
the great sweetness of a light passed
and that was enough to ignite a sky made gold
by the compassion and joy surrounding the wilderness
    of your hair

Nel bosco

e tu pensavi che come a un saggio orientale
ti bastasse stare addossato a gambe incrociate
alle radici sporgenti di un faggio
per allontanare il pensiero di lei
e diventare l'azzurro tra i rami
o magari formica corteccia filo d'erba

sono passati tre lenti fiocchi di nuvole
e sei ancora tu

ami, ma ami senza:
migliore esperienza?

In the Woods

And you had thought it would be enough
to lean cross-legged like an eastern sage
at the protruding roots of a beech tree
to distance the thought of her
and become the blue between the branches
or maybe an ant, bark, blade of grass.

Three tufts of clouds have passed
and you're still you –

you love, but you love without...
the best way?

Grafologia di un addio

Questo azzurro di luglio senza te
è attraversato da troppi neri rondoni
che hanno un colore di antenne
e il taglio, il guizzo della tua scrittura.
Si va dal "caro" alla firma
dal cielo alla terra
dalla prima all'ultima riga
dai tetti alle nuvole.

Sketch of a Farewell

The gentian blue of this July without you
is crossed by too many black swifts
the color of aerials
with the style, the dart, of your handwriting.
It goes from the "dear" to your signature,
from the sky to the earth,
from the first line to the last,
from the rooftops to the clouds.

Istria

Pietra su pietra
poveri muri a secco senza calce
pazienza di secoli
frutti color delle foglie
doline color dell'amore
con quel po' d'acqua che basta
perché attorno al tuffarsi delle mantidi
si allarghino perfettissimi cerchi;
nelle ore calde della giornata
la gente sta seduta
le mani in mano sulla porta di case,
un gatto gioca col topo
nella polvere della strada di Albona,
una donna cala il secchio nel pozzo
lo ritira fin quasi a metà
lo riaffonda di nuovo...
Non pensavo che si potesse fare una lettura
dei segni di questa terra assonnata.

Istria

Stone on stone
poor, dry walls without lime
patience of the centuries
fruit the color of leaves
ravines the color of love
with just enough water
so that all around the dives
of plunging mantises perfect rings enlarge.
In the hot hours of the day
people stay in their chairs
hands in their laps, at the door of the house.
A cat plays with a mouse
in the dust of a street in Albona.
A woman lowers a pail into the well,
pulls it back halfway,
lowers it again...
I didn't think one could read
the signs of this drowsy earth.

Casa nuova

Vi si incrociano strade
che vengono da lontano
e non si sa dove vanno.
La mia spada aveva un nome nuovissimo
ho dato un tal colpo
che è entrata a metà nella grande radice
spianata a forma di tavolino
con cui l'architetto aveva arredato il soggiorno
gli architetti si sa
ma la spada non è piú riuscita.
Lettore di neve fradicia
sia chiaro che questa spada non è un simbolo
    di quello che credi
ti ripeto, aveva un altro nome,
un vecchissimo nome.

New House

The streets coming from far off
cross each other
so you can't tell where they're going.
My sword had a very new name.
I struck such a blow
that it went halfway into a large root
flattened to make it a table
the architect had used to furnish my livingroom.
We all know how architects are
but the sword never came out.
Reader of rubbish
it should be clear this sword is not a symbol
    of that which you believe.
It had another name, I tell you,
a very, very old name.

Il pubblico e il privato

È entrato aprile in casa con il merlo
che fischia sopra i fili del bucato
è entrato in città il vento ed è passato
sui prati piú ingialliti, sotto i ponti
di ferro, come un volo per scommessa
di un biplano dei primi aviatori.
Sulle spallette della sopraelevata
dove uomini in blu hanno fissato
dei lunghi cassoni di cemento
per piantare del verde e qualche fiore
e far piú umana la grande città
(ma se neppure un'erba selvatica
ha voglia di attecchire e di fiorire
nei vasi del sindaco sociale!)
il vento ha spazzato tutto quanto
sollevato la polvere e la terra
e ora alza bandiere sui pennoni
laggiú alla fiera internazionale.
Piú tardi quando chiudono i mercati
e vanno donne con fresche verdure
(sgusceranno piselli ai ballatoi
tra piante color delle viole
fiorite in pentole smaltate di blu)
mi sembra ruoti il disco solare
tra i tetti di un'altra città.

anni 1960-70

The Public and Private

April entered the house with the whistle
of a blackbird above the washlines.
Wind entered the city and passed –
over the yellow fields and under the iron
bridges – like a biplane flight
bet on by early aviators.
On the parapets of the overpass,
men in jeans have hung
long cement windowboxes
to plant a few green scrubs and some flowers
in order to make the metropolis more humane
(although even weeds don't
want to grow nor flowers bloom
in vases of the socialist mayor).
The wind has swept it all away,
lifting a little dust here, a little earth there,
now raising flags above the yards
at Milan's annual International Fair.
Later, when the markets close
and women leave with fresh vegetables
(some shelling peas on the balcony
between purplish plants
flowering in blue enamel pots),
the solar disc seems to wheel
through the skyline of some other city.

1960-70

Congedo

Tenerissimo yeti te ne andrai dunque
in una casa di pietra serena
nascosta sopra il lago tra gli abeti.
So che mi mancherai quando piú vuoti
volgono i cieli ma non torna stagione
e nel piombo dell'aria anche è un silenzio
il tuo lungo fruscío sui tappeti.
Poi piove piove e sotto la grondaia
l'acqua scende a formare un rivoletto
che corre via sulle lastre di ardesia.
Passa una ragazzina col fazzoletto
viola annodato al collo, vai d'accordo
col suono dei suoi zoccoli olandesi.

1975

Leaving

My very gentle yeti, you'll leave soon
yes, but to a gray stone house
hidden beyond the lake and between the firs.
I know I'll miss you when the empty skies
change and the season doesn't
and there's a silence in the leaden air.
Your rustle will linger over the carpets.
Then it will rain. It will rain
and under the gutter the water will form a stream
that runs clear onto the sheets of slate.
When a little girl passes with a purple
scarf tied at her neck, it will be your absence
echoing the sound of her Dutch clogs.

1975

Il roccolo

Su uno sperone di monte cresceva
un'erba né gialla né nera
un casotto neppure si vedeva
verde tra faggi e betulle
né lontani né troppo vicini
finché da una feritoia partí un colpo
a apparve un lungo essere nero
a raccogliere un uccellino caduto da un ramo secco
un essere come quei magri che nei western portano
    un cilindro
e fabbricano casse da morto sulla main street:
ma questo era bergamasco e coadiutore
e se vado ancora per preti
è piú che mai per una questione di equilibri
direi qui per un gusto di colori
di verde di polenta e di nero.
Che sei poi volete saperne di piú
andate a trovare il Pfarrer Johann Hämmerle
che in una certa valle delle Alpi
coltiva fiori di altissimo stelo
di petali azzurri e stellati:
devo dire che il miele delle sue api ha un sapore sui
    generis.
Pare che questi fiori
(ma chi si fida dei preti?)
siano stati trapiantati da non so qual pianoro dell'Asia
    Centrale.

Bird Trap

A grass neither yellow nor black
grew on a mountain peak;
there was a hut you couldn't quite see
painted green between beech and birch trees
which were neither far away nor very near;
then there was a blast from a hole
and a tall black creature emerged
and picked up a small bird fallen from a dry branch,
a creature like those thin guys in westerns who wear
    top hats
and build coffins on Main Street.
But this one was from Bergamo, a coadjutor.
If sometimes I look up priests
it's a question of equilibrium.
I'd say here it's a matter of colors:
green-cornmeal-black.
If you want to know more
go find Pfarrer Johann Hämmerle
who lives in a certain valley of the Alps
and grows long-stemmed flowers
with blue, star-shaped petals.
I have to admit the honey of his bees
    has an incomparable taste.
It seems these flowers
(but then who believes priests?)
were transplanted from who-knows-which plateau of
    Central Asia.

Tristi giochi di parole

su uno sfondo di muri giallini
cespi di tagetes e fogliuzze rotonde
che spuntano da minimi cerchi di terra
attorno ai giovani tassi di un ospizio:
il sole non fu mai cosí mite
su queste bianche sedie di vecchie.
Un giorno arriva una lettera tassata
invita a ritirare gli "effetti personali,"
un pastrano, qualche calza spaiata
un numero incredibile di lamette di rasoio
uno spelato pennello di tasso

Sad Puns

On a background of pale yellow walls
tufts of daisies and small curved leaves
grew in small round flower beds
at bases bored with yew tree shadows.
The sun has never shown this dimly
on the white chairs of the aged.
One day a stamp boring into a "postage due" letter
asks you to pick up some "personal effects":
an overcoat, some unmatched socks,
an incredible number of razor blades,
and a worn boar-bristle brush.

Richiudendo un baule

Quel berrettuccio di lana vergine
bianco grigio e marrone
comprato in un folto di abeti
da un'indiana della riserva Sioux
(starà bene alla seconda bambina
che ha un taglio d'occhi un po' samoiedi)
anni dopo lo ritrovo in fondo a un baule
di un'umida casa in campagna.
Neppure messo una volta
sembra ora un passato di castagne
quasi un mont-blanc, ma seduto.
E dire che l'indiana aveva sorriso
accarezzato il cavallo
e che il sole tra gli alberi...
Ma addio Montagne Rocciose
hand knitted original article!

1975

Relatching a Trunk

I found that stupid white, gray
and brown cap of virgin wool
bought from the Sioux Indian
at the reservation in a clump of firs
(it would look good on my second child
with almond eyes)
years later in the bottom of a trunk
in a damp country house.
Not even worn once,
by now it could almost be chestnuts
ground for a cake that's fallen.
And to think that the Indian had smiled,
stroked my horse,
and that the sun between the trees...
so much for that Rocky Mountain
"hand-knitted original article!"

1975

Suite americana

C'è da dire
che eravamo entusiasti del nostro nuovo cappello di
    pelo
sulla diagonale spazzata dal vento
né del tutto infelici
tra tavoli bisunti di salsicce
inondati di birra, sopra il ferry,
che si andasse all'ovest o verso est.
La bambina biondo oro
in corsa sull'ammezzato
rischiosamente vicino a balconate di ferro battuto
che davano su una hall piena di luci
e i palmizi di un grande magazzino
non ne sa niente, non ricorderà
la pista nel bosco, cancellata
dalle betulle cadute di traverso,
e neppure tutte le rughe del vecchio hardware di N.B.
che si spianavano al solo vederla
mentre mi vendeva chiodi di diversa misura.
Un mattino arriva un merlo di tre colori
un merlo d'oltremare
che m'invita a tornare.

1978

American Suite

You could say
we were excited about our new fur hat
on a windy Broadway
not totally miserable
between tables greasy with sausage
inundated with beer on the ferry
whether it was going west or east.
My golden-blond girl
running across the mezzanine
dangerously close to the wrought iron rail
overlooking a hall filled with the lights
and palms of a department store
knows nothing – will not remember
the trail in the woods, erased
by the birches fallen across it,
nor all the wrinkles of the old
hardware salesman at N.B. that smooth at the sight
of her as he sells me different sizes of nails.
One morning a three-colored blackbird appears,
a blackbird from overseas,
insisting I return.

1978

Quartiere Solari

Milano ha tramonti rosso oro.
Un punto di vista come un altro
erano gli orti di periferia
dopo i casoni della "Umanitaria."
Tra siepi di sambuco e alcuni uscioli
fatti di latta e di imposte sconnesse,
l'odore di una fabbrica di caffè
si univa al lontano sentore delle fonderie.
Per quella ruggine che regnava invisibile
per quel sole che scendeva più vasto
in Piemonte in Francia chissà dove
mi pareva di essere in Europa;
mia madre sapeva benissimo
che non le sarei stato a lungo vicino
eppure sorrideva
su uno sfondo di dalie e viole ciocche.

1978

Quartiere Solari

Milan has burnished sunsets.
One view was like another:
suburban gardens beyond
the big, ugly homes of the *Umanitaria*.
Between the elder hedges
and some small tin doors and unhinged shutters,
the smell of a coffee factory merged
with that of the far-away foundries.
With all that invisible rust,
with all that voluminous dusk
over Piedmont, France – who knows where –
I seemed to be in Europe.
My mother knew perfectly well
I wouldn't be near her for long
and yet she was smiling
before a background of dahlias and purple carnations.

1978

Studia la matematica!

La villetta era al capo opposto della città
vi stagnava un afrore di soffritti
il fermacarte era un bossolo di granata
andavo infatti a lezione di matematica.
La vestaglia frusciava, un po' si apriva
succhiavo assorto una matita faber
dal sotterraneo udivo il ronzío
della fresa di un marito ingegnere
capivo poco e non ricordo altro
sí, clacson nelle vie sotto cieli di piombo
e l'acne giovanile di un ritornare a zonzo.

Study Mathematics!

The cottage was at the other end of the city.
There was the pungent smell of fried food hanging in
    the air,
a paperweight that had been the shell of a bomb –
it was where I went to math lessons.
Her robe rustled, opened a little.
I was absently sucking a Faber pencil
while listening to the buzz
of the cutter in the basement that was her husband
the engineer. I understood little and remember less.
Yes, there were horns in the streets beneath heavy skies
flaring up like the youthful face of a wayward minor.

Fine delle vacanze

Ero uno che sollevava la pietra
affondata nell'erba tra la malva
scoprendo un mondo di radicole bianche
di città color verde pisello;
ma partite le ultime ragazze
che ancora ieri erano ferme in bicicletta
nascoste da grandi foglie di settembre
alle sbarre del passaggio a livello
mi sento io stesso quella pietra.
Anche le nuvole sono basse sui campi di tennis
e il nome dell'hotel scritto sul muro
a nere, grandi lettere è tutto intriso di pioggia.

Ending Vacations

I was the one who raised the stone
buried in grass between the mallow
and discovered the world of small, white roots
of pea-green cities,
but when the last girls had left
(who just yesterday were hidden
by September's great leaves, waiting
on their bicycles at the rail bar's crossing)
I felt just like that stone myself.
Clouds are also lowering over tennis courts
and the name of the hotel written on the wall
in large, ashen letters is drenched with rain.

Niagara chic

Arrendevole
finisco sempre per andare in posti sbagliati
pittori ignoti, presunti perseguitati
piú un sapientino che ci dice attention
les Brésiliens ne parlent pas l'espagnol
il vino è buono, le donne sfiorite
se una sera vale l'altra
me ne sto qui come in un guscio di noce
come chi, avessi vent'anni di meno,
si affidasse rinchiuso in una botte
alla corrente che porta a una cascata.

Niagara Chic

Giving in,
I always manage to end up in the wrong place:
unknown painters and the presumably persecuted,
then some wise guy says, *attention,*
les Brésiliens ne parlent pas l'espagnol.
The wine is good, the women are wilted –
as if one evening's as good as another.
I stay put – as in the shell of a nut
or like someone (were I twenty years younger)
who'd let himself go sealed in a barrel
to the current leading to a falls.

Abito a trenta metri dal suolo

Abito a trenta metri dal suolo
in un casone di periferia
con un terrazzo e doppi ascensori.
Questo era cielo, mi dico
attraversato secoli fa
forse da una fila di aironi
con sotto tutta la falconeria
dei Torriani, magari degli Erba
e bei cavalli in riva agli acquitrini.
Questo mio alloggio e altri alloggi
libri stoviglie inquilini
questo era azzurro, era spazio
luogo di nuvole e uccelli.
L'aria è la stessa: è la stessa?
sopravvivere: vivere sopra?
Non so come mi sento agganciato
la sera ha tempo di farsi piú blu
da un pallido re pescatore
o, di passaggio qui in alto,
dal vero barone di Münchhausen.

I Live Thirty Meters from the Ground

I live thirty meters from the ground
in a sprawling suburban complex
with a terrace and double elevators.
This was sky, I tell myself,
crossed centuries ago
maybe by a file of herons
with all the falconry below
of the Torrianis or even the Erbas
and handsome horses on the swamp's shore.
This lodging of mine and other lodgings –
books, crocks, lodgers –
this was blue sky, a space:
a place for clouds and birds.
The air's the same, or is it?
Outliving it: living it out?
I don't know how but I feel hooked
(evening still has time to deepen its blue)
by a pallid Fisher King
or just passing through up here,
by the true baron of Münchhausen.

Ho mai trovato

cercando bacche e raddrizzando torti
da questa parte nevosa delle alpi
accompagnato solo dai miei passi
accompagnato solo dai miei morti
ho mai trovato
ho mai trovato un esercito spagnolo
che per stolido scambio di persona
mi lasciasse a me stesso in fondovalle
tra spine e infiorescenze azzurre e gialle

Have I Ever Found

Looking for berries and straightening faults
on this snowy side of the Alps
I'm alone with my steps,
alone with the dead
I may never have found.
Have I ever found a Spanish army
which, for a foolish case of mistaken identity,
would leave me alone at the bottom of the valley
among thorns and blooms, yellow... blue?

Se non fosse

Se non fosse per queste piccole cifre
per queste ultime e umili cifre
un tempo si sarebbe detto centesimi
per le quali il totale delle entrate
non fa rima con quello delle uscite
e non quadra il bilancio di fine d'anno
(la nebbia sta invadendo le terrazze
ma il fumo sale dritto sopra i tetti?
gli immigranti lanciano petardi
que le blanc ne se casse, mi raccomando)
se non fosse per queste minime cifre
ma discordi, e che fanno la spia
non si starebbe a risalire i conteggi
per trovare il nodo, il principium erroris
la smagliatura, il 5 per un 6
(ma la svista era un 8 per un 3)
non si avrebbe l'eureka, né la folle discesa
per le scritture, né l'arrivo in volata
sino all'abbraccio del dare a dell'avere:
ora saltino i tappi di spumante
e sia zero anche questo
mio ennisimo dí di San Silvestro.

1978

If Not For

If it weren't for these small numerals,
for these last, humble numerals
that once would have been called cents
and thanks to which the total income
doesn't square with the expenditure
and the balance isn't balanced at the end of the year
(fog invades the terrace
but does the smoke rise directly from the roofs? –
as the immigrants launch firecrackers
I warn, "Don't forget the wine that's chilling");
if it weren't for these tiny
but conflicting numerals, one would not
review the calculations
to find the knot, the principium erroris,
the discontinuity where there's a 6 for a 5
(but the true oversight was an 8 for a 3)
nor would one have the eureka, the mad drive
through the entries, nor the final sprint
towards the embrace of assets and liabilities:
now corks of spumante pop
so let even this be zero,
my umpteenth New Year's Eve.

In Romagna

Faceva buio, era luglio, ero a Bellaria
in un villino dipinto di rosa.
Da un campo di patate appena smosso
saliva il fresco della terra scura.
Uscí un bambino da una casa lunga
o bassa, che gridava "vedo viola!"
"sarà il Violani," "ma no!, è il calomelano"
tutta sera discussero i vicini.
Tra il canneto e la strada ferrata
si vedeva la villa di Panzini.

1979

In Romagna

It was getting dark. It was July. I was in Bellaria
in a cottage painted pink.
From a just-hoed potato field
the dark earth's freshness rose.
A little boy came out of a house
either long or low and cried, "I see purple!"
"That would be the Violani." "But no, it's the calomel!"
All evening the neighbors will debate it.
Between the cane clearing and the railroad
you could see the Panzini villa.

1979

Un dubbio

ho migliaia di lettori sovietici
Ital'janskaja Lirika XX Veka, Ed. Progress
qualche decina di lettori italiani
ultimo estratto conto Mondadori
insorgono alcune perplessità
(a Milano, quando si giocava per strada,
e a Capodanno le gambe degli spinaci sembravano piú
    rosse,
tra ragazzi si diceva "Pilade, mi viene un dubbio")
insomma che dire, che fare, čto delat'?

A Doubt

I have thousands of Soviet readers –
Ital'janskaja Lirika XX Veka, Ed. Progress –
and a few dozen Italian readers.
With Mondadori's last account statement
 certain puzzling things arise
(in Milan, when we played in the street
on New Year's Day, the spinach stalks seemed redder,
one of us said to the others, "Pylades, I have a doubt")
which is to say in short, what can you do, "čto delat' "?

Se è tutto qui...

Turbano la mia limpida fede
cattolica apostolica e che piú
non tanto il corso dei tempi
il tradimento dei nuovi chierici, i magnifici scandali
mi restano in mano altri pezzi del puzzle
ad esempio il povero vitello grasso
che sarà l'unico ad andare di mezzo
quando il figliolo prodigo si deciderà a ritornare.
Chiaro che non ho capito niente
che dovrò ancora pensarci un po' su.

If This Is It...

My limpid catholic apostolic faith
is churning or what have you
not so much from the times
or betrayals of the new intellectuals, the magnificent
    scandals;
it's other pieces of the puzzle left in my hand.
For example, the poor fat calf
will be the only one to pay for it
when the prodigal son decides to return.
It's clear I haven't understood anything,
that I'll have to think on this some more.

San Martino

si dirà compleanno o genetliaco
era un mio tema sopra il re soldato
i genitori non erano d'accordo
"sai bene che il maestro"
"ma dove ho messo il mio cappello grigio"
"davanti a Dio del resto"
intanto io umile minutante padano
"andrò tardi in ufficio"
stavo a aspettare con la penna in mano
e a pensare al mio gioco del meccano

San Martino

Do you say birthday for the King's birthday, too?
My parents couldn't agree
about my "soldier king" thesis.
"You know perfectly well the teacher..."
"Now where did I put my gray hat?"
"Before God, no less."
Meanwhile I, simple padano scribe hear,
"I'll be late to the office,"
as I wait pen in hand
thinking of my game *meccano*.

L'io e il non io

diagonalmente abeti verso il cielo
mentre sopra l'abisso d'aria viola
il codafolta va di ramo in ramo
ed io con lui verso rupi rosate
mentalmente
saltellando tra me di palo in frasca

The I and the Not I

Firs diagonally cross the sky
while above the abyss in the purple air
the squirrel goes from branch to branch
and I cross the pinkish cliffs
with him mentally,
leaping myself from one subject to another.

Un giunco di palude

un giunco di palude
il fiore di prato
un campo di segala
quell'arco dove l'edera
l'abisso che suona tra gli abeti
il cerchio di schiuma
che abbraccia lo scoglio piú solo
avranno sempre dei versi, dei bellissimi versi.
Ma voi, lontani morti dei campi di sterminio?
Non ho ancora letto una poesia
che sia all'altezza del vostro olocausto.
Sarà per un'altra dimensione,
ci diremo, chissà, H_2O, mi senti?

anni 60

A Soft Swamp Wood

A soft swamp wood,
a wildflower,
a field of rye,
the arch where the ivy
and abyss sound between the firs,
the circle of froth
that embraces the ever-lonelier rock
will always have verses, beautiful verses.
But you, the distant dead of concentration camps?
I still haven't read a single poem
that does justice to your holocaust.
It would have to be spoken of
in another dimension. Who knows,
can you hear me, H_2O?

1960s

Quando penso a mia madre

Nulla ho scritto di te quando sei andata
e poco ho scritto dopo, il lungo dopo.
Ritorni solo nei sogni di ogni notte
o, il giorno, a caso, nell'aria di via B.
dopo che è nevicato e si respira;
o in una luce pomeridiana di persiane socchiuse
e vi è un fruscío di giornale di grande formato;
o in qualche nome di luogo che mi si ferma in gola.
Tutto qui? non accetto la morte, mi si dice.
È vero, non riapro i tuoi cassetti, non rileggo
le tue lettere. Che io sia
nient'altro che una pietra
un Giovannino heartless?
Quanto tempo mi resterà ancora per imparare
a sorridere e amare come te?

1978-83

When I Think of My Mother

I wrote nothing about you when you left us
and little after – the long after.
You return only in each night's dream
or by day, suddenly, in the air of B. Street
breathed in deeply after snow;
or in the afternoon light of half-closed shutters
with the rustle of newspaper pages;
or in the name of some place that sticks in my throat.
Is this it? I don't accept death, they tell me.
It's true that I don't open your drawers
or read your letters. Am I nothing
but a stone, a heartless Johnny?
How much time do I have left
to learn to smile and love as you did?

1978-83

Una visita a Caleppio

Tra donne nate per tirare carri
mi sento nascosto come un fungo
in acque basse in cerca di conchiglie
la gamba piú all'asciutto è la piú scarna
soltanto nell'immagine del padre
giovinetto, vestito da collegio,
o attento a ascoltare "Parla Londra!"
da una radio che sembra un tabernacolo
riesco e mi piace riconoscermi.
Tempo e luogo? ma forse
un novermbre di vino e di castagne;
lontano, nel silenzio della bassa,
un landò nero passa oltre le rogge,
lievi calessi accarezzano le strade
già indurite dal freddo. Gli antenati?
In cielo e in terra molte cose, Horatio...
dunque nel novero degli eventi improbabili
niente è proprio impossibile, perfino
ritrovarti, confonderci tutti
in questo mare di nebbia sulle risaie.

A Visit to Caleppio

Looking for shells in low water
among women born to pull carts
I feel as hidden as a mushroom.
It's the dry part of my leg that's skinned.
It's only the image of my father
in his school uniform
or anxious to hear "This is London!"
come from the tabernacle-shaped radio
that I manage to and want to identify with.
Time and place? Then imagine
a November of chestnuts and wine
while far away in the silence of *la bassa*
a black buggy passed
light gigs brushing the streets
already hardened by the cold. Perhaps ancestors?
In the sky and earth there are many things, Horatio...
therefore in the many improbable events
nothing is truly impossible, not even
finding you father, just as everything merges
in a sea of fog over miles of fields of rice.

Implosion

Dicembre mi ha dischiuso una finestra
nel giro che fa il Sole attorno all'Anno:
è uno spaccato freddo, ma sul fondo
vi è una tavola bianca apparecchiata.

Pranzi di Natale, ma io dov'ero?
a destra del nonno socialista?
abbiamo tutti un nonno socialista
il mio diceva "l'Odio è stolto" e aggiungeva
a noi rivolto "Ombre dal volo breve!"
(sulle guance
quando uscivamo nel cielo blu notte
rabbrividiva un'ultima arancia).

Il cerchio è aperto, la tavola ha una falla
lo spiraglio è più bianco meno freddo
chi cerco resta sempre alle mie spalle.

Implosion

December glimmered through a window
on the path the Sun makes around the Year.
There's a splitting cold, but a white table's been set
already at the end of the room.

Christmas dinners. But me, where was I?
To the right of my socialist grandfather?
We all have a socialist grandfather
and mine always said, "Hate is foolish!"
before turning to us to add, "Shadows of the brief flight!"
(a final orange tinge shivered
on our cheeks
when we went out into the blue night sky).

The circle's open. There's an empty space at the table.
It's glimmer is whiter but less cold
and the one I'm always looking for... still behind my
    shoulder.

II

THE METAPHYSICAL
STREETCAR CONDUCTOR

Ponte e città

riattraversarlo vorrebbe anche se oscilla
periglioso, sospeso sull'abisso
non importa se manca qualche asse
tra le corde stanche e sfilacciate
se il vento che soffia nella gola
fa trepido e incerto il suo passaggio
vorrebbe metter piede all'altra sponda
sponda come? di un'erba calpestata
un po' verde, un po' gialla, di città
di sobborgo, non landa né steppa
quali umani? se stesso nei passanti
per vie di pioggia, di negozi chiusi
tra facciate notturne di finestre
illuminate di ussari, di musiche
né mai chiedersi a un angolo di strada
ed io, io, ospite di quale sera?

City and Bridge

Crossing it again eventhough it sways
would be dangerous, hanging over the abyss.
It doesn't matter if some planks are missing
between the frayed and raveling cords,
if the wind in the gorge
makes the crossing anxious and unsure.
He still wants to land on the other bank.
But what bank? One with the trampled grass
of a city or its suburbs a bit green
a bit yellow – neither moor nor steepe –
and with which humans? He passes himself
with those on the rainy streets of closed stores
between nocturnal facades,
windows lit with hussars and music
never asking himself
at the corner of the street:
and I? ...I am the guest of which evening?

Nuvole

Per anni ho guardato le nuvole
a oriente di questa terrazza
senza curarmi se fossero
diverse per chi le avesse osservate
da un'altra parte della città.
Ma oggi è un giorno al duale
amo, dunque io sono, io e te siamo.
"Cara, se guardi sopra Porta Venezia
c'è una nuvola che ha la faccia di Lincoln."
Lei mi risponde al telefono
"la mia nuvola ha la faccia di Marx."

Sfrangiate nuvole
restate nuvole!

Clouds

For years I watched the clouds
from the eastern side of this terrace
without caring whether they would be
different for someone who watched them
from another part of the city.
But today exists as a day in the dual tense I love:
I am, I and you are.
"Dear, look up above Porta Venezia,
there's a cloud with Lincoln's face."
She answers on the phone,
"My cloud has Marx's face."

Frayed clouds,
stay clouds!

Viaggiatori

È un giorno di bianchi pennacchi
di fumo stampato sul cielo
da un vento che parta la neve
e arrossa le mani dei preti

è un prato un po' fuori città
tra cose in uso e in disuso
tra case senza balconi
e un margine di ferrovia

vi asciugano molte lenzuola
con panni di vari colori
dal viola a lievissimi rosa

vi corre accanto il mio treno
annoto: bucato sui fili
piú altri segnali femminili.

Travelers

It's a day of white plumes,
of smoke stamped on the sky
and of the wind that brings snow
and reddens priests' hands;

it's a field just outside the city
between things abandoned and not,
between houses without balconies
and the railway's gravel shoulder.

Many sheets are drying there
with many-colored clothes
ranging from purple to a very light rose

I note as my train travels past
the wash on the lines
along with other feminine signs.

Arcimboldi

i tuoi occhi sono prugne del nord
i tuoi denti mandorle amare
il tuo seno una doppia albiccocca
due pesche noci i tuoi fianchi
un ficodindia il tuo grembo

il mio cuore è un'anguria emiliana

Arcimboldi

your eyes are northern plums
your teeth are bitter almonds
your breasts, a pair of apricots
two ripe nectarines, your hips
a prickly pear, your lap

and my heart's a watermelon, split open!

Filo di ferro

mi hanno detto che sono un filo di ferro
perché magro svelto resistente
invece no e lo sapevamo da ragazzi
che per spezzare un filo di ferro
se non hai pinze basta piegarlo di qua
e poi di là tre quattro sei volte
cosí mi chiedo davanti a una parete
se non sia oggi la mia settima volta
una parete dove il suo profilo
non si modella piú, non si delineano
alla luce serale della lampada
la sua fronte il suo mento le sue labbra
una parete bianca

Wire

They told me I'm like a wire:
thin, slick, tough.
But since we were kids we've known
that without pliers a wire can break
just by bending it like this, like that –
three, four, six times.
So before this wall I ask myself
if today is the seventh time –
this wall where her shadow is
not shaped anymore. You can't trace
in the evening's lamplight
her forehead to her lips or chin.
Just a wall's blank.

La mantellina

Se tu sapessi come si allarma
senza ragione il cuore
quando scendi di corsa le scale di casa
avvolta nella tua mantellina nera e grigia.
Se ora sto a chiedermi dove andrai
che farai, quando ritornerai
sarà perché ricordo che ai miei tempi
la mantellina era un capo di viaggio
(o ai tempi della Primula Rossa?)
La tua breve uscita, la tua lunga assenza
mi fa passare la mano sul volto
guardare lunghi tetti di case
sentirmi come se fossi investito
da una fredda folata di nevischio.

The Cape

If you only knew the alarm
that goes off in my heart without reason
when you rush down the stairs
wrapped in your black and gray cape!
If I'm wondering now where you'll go,
what you'll do, when you'll return,
it's because in my day, I remember,
a cape was a garment for travel
(or was it in the days of Primula Rossa?).
Your brief exit, your long absence
makes me stroke my face
and look at long roofs of homes
feeling as if I were wrapped
in a freezing gust of sleet.

Seguivo il tuo viaggio

seguivo il tuo viaggio
provavo le tue impressioni
pensavo i tuoi pensieri
meglio del simulatore di un centro spaziale
che riproduce a terra le vicende
di un'astronave in volo tra le stelle
finché scese le ombre sopra i tetti
te addormentata, perso ogni contatto
caddi di quota, riabitai un mio baratro
tra voci inascoltate e la spezzata
illusione di un filo che legasse
non solo a te ma a ogni cosa sperata
ai grandi assenti, a eterni *invisibilia*

I Was Following Your Trip

I was following your trip.
I was feeling your impressions.
I was thinking your thoughts
better than a space center's simulator
reproduces on earth what happens
on a spaceship in flight between stars.
Until shadows fall on the roofs,
asleep, you had lost all contact ,
had lost height, lived again in some void
between unheeded voices and the broken
dream of a thread that would tie me
not only to you, but to all the desired,
to the great absences – the eternal *invisibilia*.

Il tranviere metafisico

Ritorna a volte il sogno in cui mi avviene
di manovrare un tram senza rotaie
tra campi di patate e fichi verdi
nel coltivato le ruote non sprofondano
schivo spaventapasseri e capanni
vado incontro a settembre , verso ottobre
i passeggeri sono i miei defunti.
Al risveglio rispunta il dubbio antico
se questa vita non sia evento del caso
e il nostro solo un povero monologo
di domande e risposte fatte in casa.
Credo, non credo, quando credo vorrei
portarmi all'al di là un po' di qua
anche la cicatrice che mi segna
una gamba e mi fa compagnia.
Già, ma allora? sembra dica *in excelsis*
un'altra voce.
Altra?

The Metaphysical Streetcar Conductor

It comes back sometimes, the dream in which
I manoeuver a streetcar without tracks
between fields of potatoes and fig trees.
Wheels don't sink into the plowed ground.
Veering around scarecrows and sheds
I go to meet September on my way to October.
The passengers are my dead family members.
As I wake up, the ancient doubt returns:
did this life not by chance just happen?
Are we just talking to ourselves,
using make-shift questions and answers?
I believe. I don't believe. When I believe
I'd like to bring with me to the hereafter
a little of this side, also the scar
marking my leg that keeps me company.
Right, and so? Another voice
seems to say *in excelsis...*
And another?

L'ippopotamo

forse la galleria che si apre
l'ippopotamo nel folto della giungla
per arrivare al fiume, ai curvi pascoli
di foglie nate a forma di cuore

forse il varco tra alberi e liane
gli ostacoli divelti, le improvvise
irruzioni d'azzurro nelle tenebre
su un umido scempio di orchidee

forse questo e qualsiasi tracciato
come a Parigi la Neuilly-Vincennes
o l'umile "infiorata" di Genzano

o un canale di Marte, altro non sono
che eventi privi d'ombra e di riflesso
soltanto un segno che segna se stesso

The Hippopotamus

Maybe the path opened by the hippo
on his way to the river through the thick jungle
and to sweeping pastures with leaves
born into the shape of a heart,

maybe the opening between trees, liane
and uprooted obstacles in the sudden
raids of blue on the darkness
above his sultry slaughter of orchids,

maybe this track as well as others
like the Neuilly-Vincennes in Paris
or the modest *infiorata* of Gensano,

or even the canal on Mars are nothing
but shadowless events that reflect
just a sign signifying itself.

III

ELSEWHERE

La vida es

(rileggendo il Parini)

La corsa allegra del trasporto pubblico
il pie' non dubitante a curve e arresti
la stessa calca, se una donna sorride,
fasciati di cretonne gli arditi fianchi,
tanto basta all'anziano passeggero
per sentirsi rivivere un istante
(ma anche un coro di Verdi o certa luce
tra le foglie ai giardini della Guastalla).

Né se un giovine onesto dice "prego
s'accomodi," è gran male perché il gioco
delle parti è previsto e manifesto
anzi l'anziano prende posto fiero
di questa ritrovata dignità
nel balletto degli usi e dei costumi.

Ma se a dire "s'accomodi" è un teppista
o peggio uno di quelli che vorrebbero
cambiare il mondo con barba e bisaccia,
l'invito suona come una sentenza
di morte senza appello. Le mie rughe,
si dice il passeggero, il crin canuto,
le mie spalle cadenti hanno commosso
perfino questo pseudo proletario.

La Vida Es...
(rereading Parini)

The merry race of public transport,
the sure foot at the curving bends
and stops, the very crowd itself –
if a woman smiles whose daring hips
are wrapped by a fabric belt –
are all enough for an elderly passenger
to feel he's alive again for a moment
(or also a Verdi chorus or certain lights
between the leaves in the Guastalla gardens).

It's not so bad if an honest young man
says, "Please be seated,"
because the role-playing is expected
and clear. In fact, the elderly man
will take his place with pride in his renewed
dignity in the ballet of costumes and customs.

But if the one who says, "Be seated,"
is a hooligan or worse – one of those
who hopes to save the world with a knapsack and beard –
the invitation sounds like a death sentence
without appeal. "My wrinkles,"
the passenger would say, "my white hair
and sloping shoulders have moved
even this pseudo-proletarian."

E perché tutto torni come prima
il sole il mondo l'oggi e l'illusione
occorre che frenando il mezzo pubblico
il giaccone verdastro dell'irsuto
s'accoppii coi fiori del cretonne
nella valle di Giosafat di un autobus
in corsa, giallo, sotto gli ippocastani.

And for things to go back to as it was before –
the sun, the world, the dream that is today –
the greenish jacket of the unkempt man
should mate with the flowers of the fabric belt
in the Giosafat Valley yellow bus
speeding along under chestnut trees.

La lumaca

cochlea
quindi palatalizzazione
geminazione
attrazione sull'iniziale
seriore palatalizzazione mediana
chiocciola infine.
Dalle mie parti si e sempre detto lumaca.
Sbagliando sí, è con questo?
voglio dire, se la bresciana
per filogenesi avesse ereditato
quella maniera di adesione alle cose
e l'indugio sapiente
tra i fili d'erba e le foglie piú fresche!
se il milanese avesse saputo
valicare mura e bastioni
scalare alte inferriate
portare notizie di bosco
raccontare ogni goccia di rugiada
svelare i sogni piú inconfessabili
che appaiono di primo mattino
quando all soglia di un tempio di marmo
si arresta la lunga pista argentata!

anni 60

The Snail

Cochlea
and therefore palatalizzazione,
gemination –
the initial attraction
of ulterior, median palatalizzazione;
finally, chiocciola.
Where I live, they always said *lumaca*.
It's a mistake, yes? And so?
I mean, if only the Brescia girl
had inherited by philogeneses
that sort of adhesion to things
as well as a skilled lingering
in the grasses and the freshest leaves!
If only the Milanese had known
how to scale bastions and walls
and how to climb iron-railed heights
to bring news of the woods
and tell about each drop of dew,
revealing the most inadmissable dreams
that surface at dawn
when the long, silver trail stops
at the threshold of a marble temple!

1960s

Irreversibilità

Fu piú di un grido: Coglili col gambo lungo!
ranuncoli doppi, ranuncoli gialli
dove il fiume rinasce
sull'argine si cammina tra due acque.
Piú di un grido e altre albe
quando il diamante assai raro
sanguina nei vapori di aprile
sul sonno di una nuova città.
Aspettami!
Ti se allontanato tra i noccioli.

1963

Irreversibility

It was more than a cry: gather the long-stemmed!
There were doubled buttercups, yellow buttercups
where the river appears
on the bank that you walk on between two waters.
More than a cry and other dawns
when the very rare diamond
bleeds into April's vapors
on the sleep of a new city.
Wait for me!
You're already deep within the hazelnut grove.

1963

Quale pianeta?

Sempre, i prati sono piú alti di noi
o è una strada tra baracche sotto la neve
o la pianura: mi fermo a una stazione di servizio
fiorita di campanelli bianchi e viola
di nuovo mi fermo e il rampicante
si dissecca sul chiosco dipinto
è interrotto continua si attorciglia
offre tutti i suoi semi, la pianura
nel cielo terso, sotto il vento teso
non ha piú verde fino ai monti lontani.

1963

Which Planet?

The fields are always above us.
Either it's a road between barracks under snow
or plains. I stop at a gas station
with flowers of white and violet bells.
I stop again and the creeper
has dried out on the painted kiosk.
Interrupted, it continues to twist itself,
offers all its seeds. The plain
of clear sky under a taut wind
has no more green until the distant mountains.

1963

Quale Milano?

La cartolina tra i raggi della ruota
imitava un suono di motore
quando in via XX Settembre
si scendeva dal Parco in bicicletta:
perché a Milano, per biliardo che sia
vi sono strade in salita e in descesa
piú frequenti nei sogni e nei ricordi
specie se legate a un primo incontro
a un saluto guantato di viola.

Which Milan?

The postcard in the wheel's spokes
imitated the sound of motors
when you sped down from the park
towards Via XX Settembre by bike
since Milan, flat as a pooltable itself,
has both inclining and declining streets
more frequently seen in memories and dreams –
especially if they remind you of a first encounter
with a waving purple glove.

L'altrove

Perché gli spazi intermedi
i vani regni di sonno e di assenza
che si attraversano fuori città
diretti a mete di monte e di fiume

i tracciati per strade e viali
dove il verde dei platani è quasi grigio
davanti a ville dove altre le aiole
il verde dei cedri del Libano è quasi nero

perché i tratti di cielo sull'Atlantico
sulla maggioranza silenziosa delle nuvole
tra irlande verdi e grigie terre nuove

o il tempo che il bianco mi nasconde
tra due scatti di rami di un abete
se la neve si stacca dalle fronde?

Elsewhere

Why these intermediate spaces,
the vain kingdoms of absence and sleep
that one crosses out of town
going in the direction of mountains and rivers –

the tracings through streets and avenues
where the green of plane trees is almost gray
in front of villas where, beyond flowerbeds,
the green of Lebanon cedar is almost black;

why the expanses of sky above the Atlantic
on the silent majority of clouds
between Ireland-greens and Newfoundland-grays

or the time that whiteness hides from me
when, between two branches that spring,
the snow fell from their needles?

Motus in fine velocior

anche tu aspetti il fischio dell'arbitro
come quei calciatori
che ottenuto un vantaggio di reti
rallentano il gioco in attesa
che scada il tempo della partita
non ti ha insegnato niente la tua squadra
quella che stava vincendo
scendeva la nebbia sullo stadio
e fu veloce, anzi piú veloce alla fine
era l'Inter
una volta tanto.

Motus in fine velocior

You also wait for the referee's whistle
just as those players,
having gained the advantage of goals,
slow the game
to wait for the final minutes to end.
Your team didn't teach you anything,
the one that was winning.
The fog simply lowered over the stadium
and they were fast, even faster then –
it was Inter
in the end.

Autoritratto

Uomo vecchio in città
disperso su tronchi secondari di ferrovia
o con un piatto di lesso
davanti a tetti umidi di pioggia.

Tutto qui il tuo qui e ora?
Interroghi l'alfabeto delle cose
ma al tuo non capire niente di ogni sera
sai la risposta di un mazzo di rose?

Rimani quello che andava per ciliege
e a mani vuote
strappava al tronco nastri di corteccia.

Resti un ladro di polli
con gli occhi oggi ancora sprovveduti
di quando in ritardo andavi a scuola.

Self-Portrait

Old man in the city, missing
on minor railway sections
or with a plate of boiled meat
facing the damp roofs of rain,

is this it: you're here and now?
You question the very alphabet of things
but can you answer the "not-understanding-anything"
    at night
or know what response might rise from a bouquet of
    roses?

You're still that boy who went for cherries
and, empty-handed,
ripped strips of bark from the tree.

You remain the chicken thief
with eyes still as desperate
as when you left for school too late.

Notes

"If I Ever Remember You": *Illyrian:* In antiquity, Illyria was the eastern seaboard of the Adriatic. As the western half of what was Yugoslavia and northern Albania, its interior frontier was never clearly defined. The eyes, then, would suggest mysterious and exotic origins.

"New House": *novissimi:* This term is meant to register the weight of the judgement at death concerning heaven or hell.

"Leaving": *yeti:* This is the name of a kitten born in the Erba house with a deformation of the spine that caused him to lumber and run awkwardly – giving the appearance of a miniature abominable snowman. He eventually died in a peaceful villa overlooking one of the northern Italian lakes.

"Bird Trap": *casotto:* Not just a hut, but a camouflaged location where hunters wait for unsuspecting prey.

"Sad Puns": *tassi – tassata – pennello di tasso:* Homophony in the previous series of words exists in the original and has been altered to the *bore – bored – boar-bristle* series in this version to replicate the original's effect.

"Quartiere Solari": *Umanitaria:* The name of a socialist project in one of Milan's suburb's, this refers to the construction of affordable housing in abandoned areas and the tenants attempting to extend the project.

"Study Mathematics!": *ritornare a zonzo:* As a totally invented phrase, this implies a contradiction of terms similar to "marrying alone."

"I Live Thirty Meters from the Ground": *barone di Münchhausen:* This is the name of the protagonist of the novel written by R. E. Raspe in 1785. One of the extraordinary tales he told was of walking through the sky on a cannonball. The poet imagines the baron also passing through his mind's sky, giving the poet access to the fantastic.

"In Romagna": *Violani/calomelano:* Calomelano refers to mercury chloride and Violani is the name or mark of the pharmacy that produced it. *Panzini villa:* Alfredo Panzini (1863-1939) was a noted Italian writer and lexicographer. His dictionary, which went through many editions, was noted for its inclusion of slang.

"A Doubt": *Pilade:* Taken from a rather racy story, this was what the poet and his teenage friends called each other when suggesting the other couldn't be believed *čto delat':* The original title of Lenin's famous work, it simply stated what was to be done to create a new strategy for Bolshevism.

"If This Is It…": *nuovi chierici:* Taken from Julian Benda's *Le Trahison des Clercs* of 1927, this refers to the position that current intellectuals or "i nuovi chierici" have politicized their projects at the expense of artistic value.

"San Martino": *il re soldato:* Italian textbooks gave King Vittorio Emanuele this name, presumably to inspire patriotism in Italian youth. He was also born on San Martino, making it his *genetliaco* or "name day." *padano:* As an adjective, this references those living in the Po basin or plain region of Italy. *meccano:* Corresponding to the English *leggos*, this game is described as, "a building system with parts that can be fitted together to make almost anything, and then rapidly disassembled to build something else."

"A Visit to Caleppio": *Parla Londra!:* This was the title of a BBC wartime transmission, which was in the original *London Speaking!* The poet images his father listening to the program turned down very low because Italian authorities severely prohibited listening to it at the time. *la bassa:* An excellent farming region outside of Milan. *In the sky and earth*: clearly taken from *Hamlet, Act I, vv. 166-167.*

"The Cape": *Primula Rossa: The Scarlet Pimpernel* in English, this was a novel about a gentleman who helped aristocrats and counter-revolutionaries in their fight against terror during the French Revolution.

"I Was Following Your Trip": *invisibilia:* Basic to the Christian faith, this term represents the Latin term for all that is spiritual.

"The Hippopotamus": *"infiorata" di Genzano:* A celebration in a small town to the north of Rome in which designs are created with beds of flowers.

"La vida es…": *la vida es…:* A title taken from Calderon de la Barca's masterpiece, *La vida es sueno.*

"The Snail": *lumaca/chiocciola:* It should be noted that in the original there is a transformation from the etymologically "low" terminology that links lumaca to *limo* or *lombrico* (earthworm) eventually to the more attractive roots that chiocciola has to *conchiglia* (seashell).

"Motus in fine velocior": *motus in fine velocior:* This is the latin term for the principle that movement gains momentum towards the end and may be used in this case as a metaphor for aging. On a more literal level, *Inter* was the Milan soccer team that tended to be supported by the bourgeoisie, with its rival *Milan* having the support (at least at the time the poet refers to) of the general population and intellectuals supporting "the people."

Afterword

The "international geography" located in Luciano Erba's work by Pier Vincenzo Mengaldo is probably the most promising portal from which to approach the poems in *The Hippopotamus*. It is through that lens that what could be called Erba's "verbal miniatures" could realize their inherent breadth and dimension. Mengaldo describes this particular geography as "un po' da chierico vagante, un po' fantastica, dove Parigi, Londra e Milano si alternano con pure località..."[1] It is in this profoundly uncertain terrain, then, that the hippopotamus so central to this collection of poems ambles on with his "sultry slaughter of orchids" through the world's jungle on his singular quest for cosmic meaning. It's the same terrain in which "the mad drive through entries" of the past year's expenditures and its barely perceptible errors in the poem "If Not For" takes place before exploding with the spumante's pop at the year's end and the poet's decision to settle on the at once vague and potent final word "umpteenth." Potentially, as seen in "Niagara Chic," it's a terrain that could take the author "sealed in a barrel to the current leading to a falls." In short, it's a shifting poetics of finely calculated risks that may have dior implications in terms of language and its expressive powers.

To continue with Mengaldo's observation, the origin of such a project can be located in a distant and unlikely geography itself – one that obliquely sets, perhaps, the glimmers of magic realism against the more somber sky of post-war realism. One of the first known appearances of the term magic realism is said to be a 1925 article written in German by Franz Roh (though later translated into Spanish and published by José Ortega y Gasset in Madrid in 1927 in the influential

Revista de Occidente). The new direction Roh locates in paint-
ing is described as a post-expressionist form indicating "that
mystery does not descend to the represented world, but rather
hides and palpitates behind it."[2] Written just three years after
Erba's birth in Milan, transferred to and published in a Span-
ish context two years later, the article seems to prefigure
Erba's antimonumental aesthetics when it claims in a section
subtitled "Smaller than Natural (Miniature)": "The *intrinsic*
miniature... is art produced by attempting to locate *infinity* in
small things... Its opposite pole is another feeling for life,
which animates monumental art..."[3] Nature's image for this,
continues Roh, is a starry sky: its tiny units or simple points
placed on the extensive context that is infinity. It is with this
precise fidelity that a celebration of the "long-forgotten and
exquisite quality of the diminutive in art"[4] can be invoked.
Thus, the reader feels Roh may speak not only for the aes-
thetic he describes but for Mengaldo's "wayward believer"
when he articulates the effect of entering certain medieval
churches that reveal – always through the minuscule – the
infinite: "On entering the church, the ensemble of an altar
painting unfolded its essential meaning at a hundred paces,
and then, as the distance diminished, revealed little by little
the new world of the very small in successive planes of details,
details that were symbolic of all true spiritual knowledge of
the world because they always remained subordinate to the
total structure. Thus the viewer could satiate himself with
minutiae, with the thickness of density of all cosmic relation-
ships."[5]

The step from this aesthetic to a new post-war approach-
ability in poetry is small indeed. Moreover, this high prioriti-
zation of the common and the daily may come to manifest
itself in the language-based medium of poetry – or may at
least set the stage for – a high valuation of the diction and pat-
terns of common speech. The moral imperative inherent in

paying attention to the minuscule, of course, involves a certain questioning of, or shift away from, dominant or conventional power structures. In terms of its revaluation of common words "of the people," it also can be seen as representing a democratization of speech.

This leads to a second useful observation made by Mengaldo: his characterization of Erba's choice of expression as "un linguaggio in via di esaurimento."[6] It's a language so subtle in its examination of the very tools the poet's required to use that it tends often to feel on the verge of its own extinction. Key words like the vital verb "shone," in fact, will be suppressed in a way that makes the image paradoxically more present, as in the line: "il sole tra gli alberi" or simply "the sun between trees." Absences, in this way, tend to figure so highly that they gain their own counterweight. They become less "absent" actually than "shaped" as an exquisitely refigured presence – one of the forces that shapes our lives, no less, unknowingly.

This becomes especially apparent as the book progresses and attempts to figure history. The schoolboy remembered at his tutorial in "Study Mathematics!" for example, senses a threat that is both acute and dim at once: beneath the seemingly benign or even dull domestic surface is the remnant of a bomb now serving as a paperweight and signaling, at the same time, some unspeakable violence that is magnified by the pungent odors of the house combined with an alarming buzzing inside the house and the jolting traffic outside of it. Historical violence, in this case, is all the more insidious for the indirect manner in which it is necessarily perceived – that is, through the unreliable yet undeniable senses of an adolescent. It is at once abstract and distinct.

It's clear, then, that "spazi intermedi" could become the natural culmination of this particular aesthetic – those silent intervals that question life's significance as well as our own

existence as they activate the conscience. Defining those diffi-
cult fissures or gaps becomes the project of the poet – describ-
ing those empty hours of solitude and their overlooked objects
where revelation may latently reside.

*

A brief return to the concept of an "international geography"
before turning to more specific choices in terms of the trans-
lations themselves would highlight the obvious influence of
French literature on Erba's work. As a professor of French lit-
erature for many years and as a scholar focusing on the sym-
bolist movement, Erba seems to have come by his linguistic
virtuosity and interest in representing the ephemeral honestly.
Moreover, he translated many French authors, including
Michaux, Ponge and Reverdy.

   Immersion in the above aesthetics may at least obliquely
link Erba to the movement in contemporary French poetry
described by John Taylor as Follain's " 'intimist' descendants."
Describing the works of François de Cornière and Gil Joua-
nard, Taylor locates a singular devotion to "humble or every-
day objects" and the detection of a "radiant 'presence' of
certain simple things" or "privileged moments." In supporting
the view of "perennial mysteries concealed in the most routine
events," Taylor continues: "Often what most intrigues is not
what the poet relates, but rather what he intentionally
omits... how to look around, wherever one is, and to place the
enigma between the lines."[7] This can be illustrated best, in
Erba's case, by the poems themselves. In "Relatching a
Trunk," it can be seen in the way an actual object found in the
trunk of a damp country house – that "hand-knitted original
article" – offered by the Sioux leads the poem instead to an
omitted sun blazing, nevertheless, so fiercely through the
Rocky Mountain's pines that the image inspires an ellipsis.

The poet finds himself without words – without words, that is, until the final and definitive "addio."

Moreover, that French *pudeur* or humility marking the project can be extended to its language, which suggests the humility of the poet's tools. Traces of both the fiercely inhabited blank spaces of André du Bouchet's *poesie blanche* and the suspenseful, halting and inclusive syntax of Philippe Jaccottet merge into a hybrid that seems to willfully wrench its presence out of a distinctly modern emptiness. The result could be said to be a tenuous power – the power of doubt. In short, the type of abyss sounding between the firs in "A Soft Swamp Wood" that's inhabited by the unbearable silence of distant holocaust victims, combined with the singular and expressive punctuation of "If Not For" as the poem races towards its own wordlessness, both set the stage for the honesty found in "The Metaphysical Streetcar Conductor" as it asks: "Did this life not by chance just happen? Are we just talking to ourselves, using make-shift questions and answers?"

*

Obviously, if this is a poetics that challenges the poet, for the translator it will be doubly so. The elusive vocabulary and syntactic slippages so characteristic of the project – the natural dislocations and evocations they create – can be seen as a part of the signature or genius of the Italian language. That quiet *dis-ease* created by its refined and fine linguistic rain can easily transform, through more concrete English equivalents, into a drenching downpour. Worse, it might even disappear into a cloudy yet ominous sky. At the risk of occasional awkwardness, I therefore tried to preserve, when at all possible, the foreign elements of the aesthetic; that is – to not just paraphrase but appropriate the words of Ortega y Gasset – "to force the grammatical tolerance of [English] to its limits in

order to carry over precisely what is not [English in Erba's]…
way of speaking."[8] This virtually transforms the translator
into an acrobat walking the fine line between what von Hum-
boldt has described as *Fremde* vs. *Fremdheit*. The first, he says,
is desirable while the second isn't. Still, the assertion made in
his introduction of his own translation of *Agamemnon* that "a
translation should indeed have a foreign flavor to it" seemed
especially apt for a poetic project as naturally cosmopolitan as
Erba's. As von Humboldt claims, "As long as one does not feel
the foreignness (*Fremdheit*) yet does feel the foreign (*Fremde*),
as translation has reached its highest goal."[9]

With that in mind, I've adopted four specific approaches to
representing the poems in English. The most obvious is
that punctuation and capitalization (in keeping with the orig-
inal) have been minimized in a way that may keep them from
being totally consistent. The Italian ability to naturally
accommodate punctuation omissions is virtually impossible at
times to replicate with English. Therefore, while the poem "If
Not For" has virtually dispensed with punctuation in the
English version to register the intended speed of time passing
in the original, punctuation has been added to "Istria" in
order to register the simple lives of the people involved and
the pace of their lifestyle. Secondly, italics are used more often
for the sake of clarity in the English versions than is necessary
in the originals. "Illyrian," for example, as a geography far less
familiar to English readers, has been italicized and kept in its
original form in order to preserve its "foreign" element –
hopefully, without registering too much "foreignness." In
terms of idioms and cultural signifiers, certain cultural trans-
fers have also been required. "Men in blue," signaling the
workman's blue *tuta* so often seen in Italy, has been repre-
sented as "jeans" in English – apparel seen just as often and
in the same context in America. Finally, linguistic transfers
were made in cases when form seemed to override content in

the original in terms of establishing the poem's meaning. That is, the word play in "Sad Puns" obviously can't be communicated with the English equivalent "badger." In order not to disrupt the imagery itself, therefore, the "tassi," "tassata" to "pennello di tasso" in the Italian has been represented as the "bore," "bored," to "boar-bristle" series in English. Most choices in terms of the translations themselves should fall into the above categories. Otherwise, I would only add that one poem in the original manuscript, "Per un lettore del terzo millennio" or "For a Reader," was deleted in consultation with the author due to its reliance on antiquated speech patterns that are incompatible with English.

It would be impossible to do justice to all the support that has contributed to this collection, as the project was initiated a decade ago in Rome and has seen numerous transformations. Various stays at the Ragdale Foundation during those years proved invaluable. The insightful earlier comments made by Richard Howard and Alfredo de Palchi's later suggestions are greatly appreciated and fondly remembered. The support and hospitality of Luciano and Mimia Erba also proved invaluable. Mimia in particular traveled untold kilometers and made heroic attempts to rescue these versions from their own faithlessness at times. Her steady eye is undoubtedly behind any successes that may exist and is certainly not responsible for any lapses that may occur. Finally, the book itself was made possible by the generous support of the Raiziss-Giop Charitable Foundation, which has my deepest gratitude.

Ann Snodgrass,
Cambridge, 2001

Notes

1. Mengaldo, Pier Vincenzo. *Poeti Italiani del Novecento*. Milan: Mondadori, 1978. 909

2. Zamora, Lois Parkinson and Wendy B. Faris, eds. *Magical Realism*. Durham: Duke University Press, 1995. 15

3. Ibid. 27

4. Ibid. 29

5. Ibid. 30

6. Mengaldo, Pier Vincenzo. *Poeti Italiani del Novecento*. Milan: Mondadori, 1978. 908

7. Taylor, John. "From Intimism to the Poetics of 'Presence':Reading Contemporary French Poetry," *Poetry*. Oct./Nov. 2000. 156

8. Ortega y Gasset, José. "The Misery and the Splendor of Translation," *Theories of Translation*. Rainer Schulte and John Biguenet, eds. Chicago: University of Chicago Press, 1992. 112

9. von Humboldt, Wilhelm. "*from* Introduction to His Translation of *Agamemnon*," *Theories of Translation*. Rainer Schulte and John Biguenet, eds. Chicago: Chicago University Press, 1992. 58

Winner of several of Italy's most prestigious awards, Luciano Erba has established himself as one of the leading Italian poets of his generation. For many years he has taught French liturature and dedicated his scholarly interests to symbolism as well as to French literature. He is translator of J. de Sponde, B. Cendrars, P. Reverdy, H. Michaux, F. Ponge and Thom Gunn along with many other French and English poets. His more than ten volumes of poetry included: *Il nastro di Moebius* (Premio Viareggio, 1980), *Il Tranviere Metafisico* (Premio Bagutta, 1988), *L'Ippopotamo* (Premio Librex-Guggenheim "Eugenio Montale"), *L'Ipotesi Circense* (1995), and *Nella terra di mezzo* (2000).

Ann Snodgrass teaches at M.I.T. She received the Renato Poggiolo Award for her translations of Vittorio Sereni from the PEN American Center.

Printed in
May 2003
at Gauvin Press Ltd., Hull, Québec